Contents

Words in **bold** can be found in the glossary

What's the story?

A story usually has a beginning, a middle and an end – it is made up of events that happen over time. Artists who want to tell a story in their works have to solve a problem: how to get the storyline across through still images. The story may be from a well-known **legend** or history, or invented by the artist.

The picture space may show just one key moment, or a whole series of events. But in every case, artists must use their skill to help the viewer to 'read' the picture: to recognize the main actors, and understand what is going on. This book explores some of the techniques and clues artists have used.

❑ Benozzo Gozzoli, **Dance of Salome**, *1461/62*

A story sequence

One way to show the action unfolding is to bring together different **episodes** from a story in the same picture. The same characters may appear more than once.

Gozzoli used this idea to tell the Bible story of the death of John the Baptist. John had criticized King Herod and his new wife. She hated John and wanted revenge. Salome, her daughter, danced for Herod at a feast. He promised to give Salome whatever she wanted in return, so, to please her mother, she asked for the head of John on a dish.

Three in one

Gozzoli manages to show in one small picture three different scenes from this story. They take place at different times in the same palace. You might think the result would be confusing. But people of his day already knew this Bible story well and he uses his art to make the **sequence** clear.

Dance of death

The central figure is the swirling Salome, dancing for King Herod at the feast. We follow her gaze to Herod. Look at Herod's expression. How does he feel about Salome's request – sad, eager or worried? Herod's guest turns to him, wondering if Herod will keep his promise. How do we know the answer? (Clue: what is he holding in his hand?)

❏ Benozzo Gozzoli
Dance of Salome (detail)

Kneeling figures

Hidden from the party to the left of the painting, John kneels while the executioner raises his sword. In an **alcove** at the rear, Salome appears again, kneeling. She places the dish with the gruesome head on her mother's lap.

In perspective

Gozzoli worked in Florence, Italy, in the fifteenth century. Artists then were studying the new science of **perspective**. They used its rules to draw scenes with a realistic feeling of depth and space. (If you follow the **diagonal** lines of the table, the walls and the ceiling, you will see that they almost appear to meet at a central point.) Gozzoli used perspective to divide and frame the different parts of the story.

A tall story

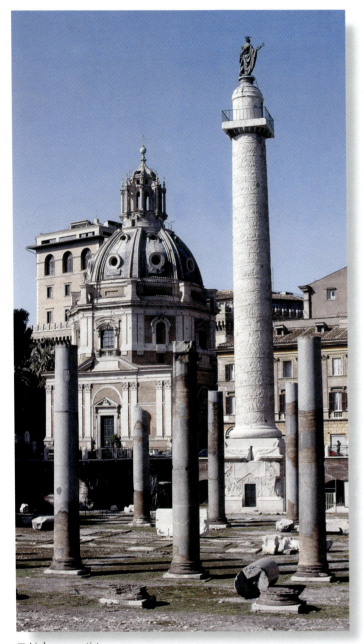

□ Unknown artists
Trajan's Column, Rome
Finished AD113
The column with its base is 38 metres tall
– about the height of a 12-storey building.

Some of the earliest stories told through art celebrate victory in war. Their main aim was to impress the viewer.

Trajan's triumph

The Roman emperor Trajan was a brilliant soldier. He won a series of victories in Dacia (today's Romania), returning to Rome with a huge amount of captured wealth. He used it to build a vast square or **Forum**, with magnificent public buildings to mark his triumph and the power of his empire.

A conquering hero

Towering over the Forum was a marble column. It is carved with a **frieze** which winds up like a long ribbon, recording the story of the conquest of Dacia. The story is told through clear and detailed images. The Roman army is shown marching and building camp, preparing food and fighting – much as television news informs us today.

Trajan himself is the **focal point** of many scenes. He is shown as one of the men rather than a superhero, but the scale of his victory could not fail to impress the public.

The view at the top

Imagine you are in the small courtyard where the column then stood. Could you 'read' the story all the way up? Even by standing on the roof of nearby buildings, it would be difficult to see it all.

- What different activities can you see in the building scene?
- How are the people dressed?
- Would a monument like this be built today? How are wars recorded and remembered nowadays?

❏ Unknown artists, **Trajan's Column (detail)**
The Roman soldiers are building **fortifications**. Notice how the sculptor shifts from a frontal view to a 'bird's-eye' view, to show inside and outside the walls at the same time. It was important to make every detail clear.

Why, then, record it in such rich detail? Perhaps one answer was found by climbing the inner staircase to the platform at the top. Looking down on the Forum, the viewer would understand that it was these hard-fought Dacian wars that had brought such splendour to Rome.

❏ Unknown artists, **Trajan's Column (detail)**
On the upper band, soldiers build a camp. Notice at the top left, one of the small rectangular windows that let light in to the internal staircase. On the lower band, the giant river god looks on as the army sets out across a bridge of boats.

Strip stories

A story can be told in a long band divided into segments. Each segment carries the action forward.

Embroidered history

The Bayeux **Tapestry** is a 70-m strip of linen, **embroidered** with wool. It tells the story of the conquest of England in 1066 by William, the French Duke of Normandy. In this section, pillars divide the story into five **frames**.

A medieval movie

The story unfolds like a film, with the action cutting from one storyline to another.

The Latin **captions**, as in a silent film, help identify people and places. Here, the key scene of Harold's coronation is like a **still**, an official photograph. In the next two frames, the action is moved swiftly forward by using the same figures twice. They show that the coronation and the comet's warning are linked. The switch to an indoor scene takes the plot a step further. The huddled whispering figures deepen the feeling of danger and suspense.

❏ Unknown artists, Detail from the **Bayeux Tapestry**
end 11th century
Odo, William's half brother and Bishop of Bayeux, had this made and hung in his cathedral in 1078, for everyone to see. It showed that William had a right to the English throne.

▲King Edward of England has died. He had promised the crown to his cousin William, but two noblemen are giving it to Harold.

▲Harold is crowned King by the Archbishop of Canterbury, and sits in state on his throne.

▲Through an open door, five onlookers cheer the new King.

▲They turn to point to an awesome sight in the sky: Halley's comet. It was thought to be an omen of disaster or war.

▲A messenger whispers to Harold. The ghostly ships in the border below hint of the fleet William is preparing for his invasion of England.

©HERGÉ/MOULINSART 2004

❑ Hergé (Georges Remi)
The Calculus Affair (detail)
1956
Tintin and Captain Haddock are investigating a
noise in a cellar, when the dog, Snowy, tumbles
down the stairs, knocking over some buckets.

The clear line

Many of these story-telling techniques are
found in modern strip cartoons nine hundred
years later. In his books about the
adventures of the fearless reporter, Tintin,
the Belgian artist, Hergé, used what he
called the 'clear line', with simple drawing
and flat unshaded colours, to tell a story.
Tintin has just a round face with two points
for eyes. Only his **quiff** of hair and baggy
trousers mark him out.

Cartoon codes

Look how, in this wordless scene, Hergé
tells a great deal through signs and marks.
• *Movement* is shown in Frame One by the
flying buckets and umbrella, and the pose
of the falling dog and startled Tintin. In
Frame Three, short repeated lines suggest
the foot kicking the pipes.

• *Noises* are written in bold letters, with
wavy sound lines.
• *Emotion* is shown through body language –
notice Snowy's dazed expression, and
Tintin's urgent hands calling for quiet in
Frame Two. His puzzled surprise is signalled
by the question mark and beads of sweat
above his head. The same marks above the
prisoner's head show anger and stress.

• Do you think the Tapestry
shares the 'clear line' style? In what ways?

• What body language do the Tapestry
figures use to make their feelings clear?
Find someone who looks worried,
confident, amazed.

A life story

Here, the events of one man's life are told in a single picture. Sir Henry Unton lived in England at the time of Queen Elizabeth I. When he died, aged only 40, Dorothy, his wife, ordered this painting to celebrate and record his life and learning.

❑ Unknown artist
The Life and Death of Sir Henry Unton
About 1596

Follow the numbered captions to see the course of Unton's life, from birth to his grand funeral.

9 Dorothy kneels ▶ behind a statue of her husband on his magnificent tomb. It was really inside the church. Why has the artist shown it outside?

▲ **8** Henry was given an especially grand funeral, because he died while serving the queen. Crowds of poor people watched the **sombre** procession. What are they doing to get a good view?

6 Henry went as the queen's **ambassador** to France, where he was taken ill. The French king's doctor looked after him.

4 He served as a soldier in the Low Countries (Belgium and the Netherlands). Where did the soldiers sleep?

• How many times does Sir Henry appear in the painting? How does the artist make him stand out?

• Imagine you are Dorothy talking about Henry. How would you describe him?

3 He travelled across the English Channel to Europe, first to Venice and Padua in Italy. What is he carrying, and why?

2 The path leads to Oxford, where Unton studied. Can you spot him in his college room?

1 Baby Henry is in the arms of his mother. She was a countess, shown by her **coat of arms** and coronet over her head.

Start here

7 Henry died, and his body was taken back to England by boat, and then by horse-drawn cart.

5 These scenes show Henry's life at home: writing, playing music, talking to scholars, and enjoying a feast with friends.

A different angle on the story

By choosing to view a scene from an unusual **angle**, an artist can show the separate threads of a story happening at the same time.

Small and detailed

This **miniature** is from a book which the great Akbar, Muslim Emperor of northern India, had painted to illustrate his reign. It tells the birth of his long-awaited first son, and the great joy of his **court** and people.

Indian painting at this time was famed for its exquisite and realistic detail. It was common for two or more artists to work together on such paintings. One might draw the **composition**, another the figures or heads, another fill in the colour.

Can you spot
- a carpet of flowers?
- a boy on his father's shoulders?
- a peacock?
- a pair of cymbals?

Inside and out

Imagine you are standing next to the artist as he paints the scene. It is as though you were looking down on it from a high window whose frame cuts off parts of the palace and the figures. From where you are, you can see everything that is going on: the birth scene in the heart of the palace, the musicians celebrating in the courtyard and the excited crowds gathering outside the walls. The angles of the palace form strong zigzag diagonals. These separate the different scenes and, at the same time, lead the eye from one to the next.

❏ Kesu Salan and Dharmadas
The Birth of Prince Salim (detail)

▶ Because of the high viewpoint, the sky and horizon are hardly visible. Notice the delicate painting of the rocks and river and the patterned palace tiles.

▶ In the stillness of an inner room, the princess Padmi rests in bed, while her maids gently wash the newborn baby.

▶ Outside, by contrast, there is a noisy explosion of joy. Vividly dressed musicians are lifting their trumpets and beating drums. Another servant holds out a great dish of spiced rice, to be given to the poor.

▶ A courtier takes coins from a deep bag to throw over the wall to the people below.

▶ Young and old, beggars and holy men throng outside. They raise their arms to greet the new prince or to catch the coins. See how their gestures echo those of the musicians above them to form a great swirl of movement.

❑ Kesu Salan and Dharmadas
The Birth of Prince Salim
About 1590

Moments of drama

An artist may choose a single dramatic moment to stand for the whole story. Such paintings usually illustrate a key point in a legend or Bible story which the audience of the time already knew well.

Sound and fury

Here, we are at the wedding feast of the Greek hero Perseus, and Andromeda, whom he had rescued from a sea monster. The princess had once been promised to Phineas, who bursts into the scene with his men to kill Perseus and claim her. Perseus pulls out his secret weapon, the ghastly snake-haired head of Medusa, that turns to stone all who look at it. Giordano organizes the scene of **climax** so we clearly know who is the hero, who is the villain and what is going on.

- How does Medusa's head stand out?
- Why is Perseus turning his head away? How would you describe his expression?
- What is happening to Phineas and his men? (Clue: look at their skin colour and poses.)
- What are the king and queen doing?

❏ Luca Giordano
Perseus Turning Phineas and His Followers to Stone
About 1680
This huge painting measures 2.75 m by 3.66 m. Compare this with the size of a wall in your home.

A Jewish heroine

This is also the story of an heroic act and a severed head – but the mood is very different. The Jewish heroine Judith saved her city from defeat by the Assyrian army. She and her servant tricked their way into the tent of the enemy general, Holofernes, and cut off his head while he slept. They carried his head back in a sack to prove that he was dead.

Deathly dark

In the darkness of the tent, Judith raises her hand as her servant stuffs the head into a sack. It is a moment of quiet but powerful suspense.

❏ Artemisia Gentileschi
Judith and Maidservant with the Head of Holofernes
About 1625

• The women fill the canvas – they seem close to us. What feeling does that give you? Do they seem calm or afraid?

• Where is the light coming from? Where does it fall? The light casts deep shadows. What effect does this give?

A story full of clues

We sometimes have to do some detective work to 'read' a picture. It can hold many clues that reveal the true story.

A moral tale

Like many artists in the nineteenth century, the English painter, Martineau, chose subjects from everyday life that tell a tale and teach a lesson. The public enjoyed them much as we do television soaps today. To us, this painting seems at first to show a tired but happy family on moving day. But a viewer of the time would know how to find and recognize the signs that tell a different story.

❏ Robert Braithwaite Martineau, **The Last Day in the Old Home**, *1862*

A man of bad habits

Sir Charles Pulleyne has been forced to sell the family home and its contents to pay his debts. A painting of a racehorse, propped on the floor, shows he has gambled away his fortune at the races. Carefree and quite unashamed, he enjoys a last drink with his young son. He is clearly passing on his bad habits.

The ruined family

His wife stretches a tired hand in despair. But it is too late now to change his ways. Their old life, like the dying fire in the grate, has reached an end.

Find the hidden meaning in the details.
Why has Martineau shown:
- bare branches tapping at the window?
- the little girl holding her doll tightly?
- old family portraits on the walls?

❏ Robert Braithwaite Martineau
The Last Day in the Old Home (details)

The family name

Behind the wineglass, the family's ancient coat of arms is carved on the fireplace. The father's drink and fast living have blackened the family name.

A sad exchange

A tearful grandmother pays the butler his last wages and he gives back the keys to the house. A newspaper advertises apartments to rent – a clue that the family's grand way of life is over.

Up for sale

All the contents of the house are being removed for sale. A list of items lies on the carpet. Pictures and furniture are marked with white numbers. (Can you spot them? There is one on the chair by the father's right knee.)

What's going to happen next?

Joseph Wright of Derby
An Experiment on a Bird in the Air Pump
1768

Like any story-teller, an artist can use suspense to capture interest. Joseph Wright, an eighteenth-century English painter, lived in an age of great scientific discovery. He was friends with the leading thinkers and inventors of the day.

He went to meetings where experiments were carried out in front of an audience, to explain the wonders and discoveries of science. It is just such a demonstration that he has chosen to paint here.

Life or death

A white cockatoo is in a glass jar attached to a pump. With one hand, the scientist pumps out the air. Unable to breathe, the bird falls. But with his left hand, the scientist holds the valve which can let air into the flask again and save the bird's life.

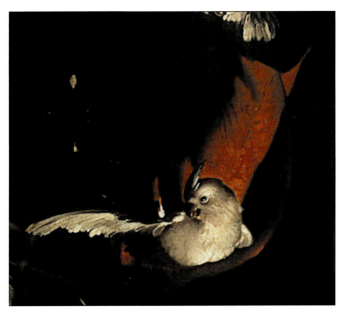

❏ Joseph Wright of Derby
An Experiment on a Bird in the Air Pump (detail)

It is truly a breath-stopping moment. The scientist looks straight out of the picture to us, his eyebrows raised as though asking a question. Should he choose to carry on with the experiment, or release the valve at the last minute? Will science or human kindness triumph? The face of the boy by the moonlit window also looks out at us. He holds a rope which will lower the cage,

so that the bird can be safely put back. Since a white cockatoo was a rare and precious bird, it was unlikely that the scientist would have killed it.

Mixed feelings

Their gazes draw us in to join the audience around the table. They are dramatically wrapped in darkness, with only the candlelight to pick out their faces and gestures. In this way, Wright focuses on their differing reactions to the experiment.

Read their expressions to see how young and old respond in different ways. Who is looking:
- fascinated?
- uninterested?
- thoughtful?
- afraid?

The two lovers on the left have eyes only for each other, while the boy next to them, and the man timing the experiment with his watch, pay close attention. A fatherly figure comforts the two frightened girls. The old man sits lost in thought, gazing at a skull in a glass jar on the table. He reminds us that this is a story not just of an experiment, but of nature's laws of life and death.

19

A story within a story

When an artist tells more than one story in the same picture, the viewer may need help to unravel the puzzle.

☐ Grant Wood
Parson Weems' Fable
1939

An American legend

In 1806, Parson Weems wrote a life story of George Washington, the first president of the USA. He told how, as a boy, George had confessed to his father that he had chopped down a cherry tree.

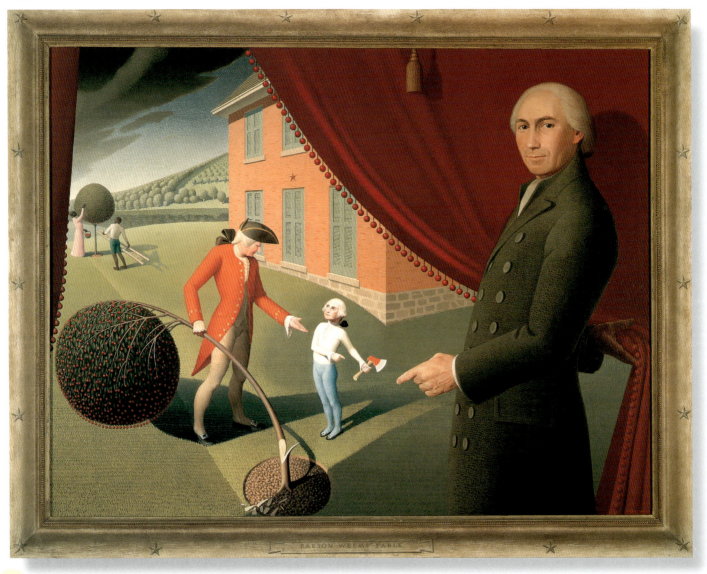

His words, 'I cannot tell a lie,' became famous, and the story became a legend. George was held up as a model of brave and honest youth. Over 100 years later, the American public was shocked to discover that Parson Weems had made the whole story up to glorify his hero. He was the one who had told a lie!

Setting the stage

Grant Wood was an American who painted in the early twentieth century. He cleverly makes fun of both the inventive parson and his **fable** in one picture. Weems himself looks calmly out at us. He holds back a curtain to point at the cherry tree scene, as though it is happening on a stage. But Wood paints the tale with a new twist of his own. It is not quite the version the public loved. The storm clouds in the sky hint at something darker.

A little rebel

The red-faced, frowning father holds out an angry hand at George. He in turn points to the guilty axe, but holds it out of his father's reach. He glares back, not at all sorry. Wood uses this play of hands and expressions in place of words. What do you think these two might be saying?

❑ Grant Wood
Parson Weems' Fable (detail)

Wood gives the little boy the head of the adult Washington as it is drawn on the American dollar bill. Why do you think he did this: so we can recognize him, or to show that the great president was really a rebel? (Washington led the **War of Independence** against the British.)

The good son

The lines of the fallen tree, the lawn and the house lead our eye to another cherry tree. A black slave shows more respect: he brings a ladder to help his mother pick fruit.

Notice Wood's storybook
style and touches of humour.
• What is the fringe on the curtain made from?
• Where else can you see these round
shapes repeated?
• What kinds of colours does Wood use
for the main scene?

A news story

❑ Dorothea Lange
Migrant Mother, Nipomo, California
1936

Since the invention of photography, images of news stories from around the world reach our homes through newspapers and magazines. These pictures may have a greater impact than words.

The Great Depression

The early 1930s were a time of crisis in the USA. Many Americans did not have jobs or homes. The American photographer, Dorothea Lange, travelled around California, taking pictures of poor farm workers who had migrated there from other parts of the USA to seek work. She used her photography to alert the government and the public to the hardship they were suffering.

Homeless and hungry

On her travels, Lange came across this **widowed** mother, Florence Owens, and her seven children, living in a tent in a pea-pickers' camp. The only things they had to eat were vegetables from the fields and birds the children killed. Lange later said of Owens, 'She seemed to know my pictures might help her, and so she helped me. There was a sort of equality about it.'

Lange took six photographs of the mother and her smallest children sitting in their makeshift tent, moving her camera in closer and closer to the scene. The other photographs show more details of their terrible living conditions. But this, the last picture in the series, is the most powerful.

- How would you describe the mother's expression? What might she be thinking?
- Why do you think the children's faces are turned away?
- Lange wanted her photographs of migrants to show 'their pride, their strength, their spirit'. Does she succeed here?
- Do you think the mother is brave or defeated?

Close up

The mother holds her baby while the others huddle around her for comfort. The camera is so close that we can see the rough texture of their shabby, grimy clothes. Owens was only thirty-two, yet she looks much older. Her face is weather-beaten from working in the fields, and lined with worry. The thin, tense hand raised to her mouth, and the haunting expression in her eyes, reveal the misery of the migrant's life.

❏ Dorothea Lange, **Migrant Mother, Nipomo, California (detail)**
What does this gesture tell about the mother's feelings?

A call for help

When Lange's photos of the family were published in the *San Francisco News*, the country was deeply shocked. The government immediately sent food aid for the starving workers. This portrait came to sum up in itself the story of the **Depression**.

Stories in the round

A story retold in sculpture can be especially vivid. Moving round the figures, seeing them from all sides, we can enter into their drama.

From Western to legend

The Senegalese sculptor, Ousmane Sow, has recreated the Battle of Little Big Horn of 1876, when the **Native Americans**, led by Sitting Bull, defeated General Custer's Seventh Cavalry.

In a panorama of twenty-four larger than life-size figures and eleven horses, the two sides charge and fall, fight and flee. All the terrible drama of the battlefield is there. However, Sow has not simply created a sculpted Western film with its 'goodies' and 'baddies'. He sees the link between the Native Americans and his fellow Africans, who also suffered as slaves at the hands of the white man. The battle becomes part of a bigger story.

❏ Ousmane Sow
The Battle of Little Big Horn – The Charge of Two Moon
1998
In this group of sculptures, the Cheyenne Chief Two Moon looms over two fallen soldiers and a tangle of dead horses.

Sow worked for many years as a physiotherapist, healing through massage. His expert knowledge and touch bring to life the veins and muscles of the Chief's strong arm and body. Sow's unusual training and technique help to make his sculptures very expressive.

Each sculpture starts with a frame of metal and wires, built on with sacking and fibres, and finally covered with a home-made paste of glue, resin and secret ingredients.

- Can you see where the different materials are visible?
- What texture do the sculptures have?
- What kind of colours does Sow use? Compare them with the Senegalese landscape where the sculptures were photographed.

❏ Ousmane Sow, **The Battle of Little Big Horn – The Charge of Two Moon (detail)**

Although Little Big Horn brought the death of Custer and victory for the Native Americans, Sow does not show it as a triumph. The bodies of the fallen soldiers are twisted with pain and fear, but we do not see blood or wounds. The pointless tragedy of war is expressed in the tangled bodies of the magnificent horses. Above them, Chief Two Moon looks down.

With his powerful, muscled body and noble head, he is like a hero in a legend. His face does not show hatred or anger. Instead, he has an expression of great dignity and sadness. It is as if he knew the victory would be short-lived: fourteen years later, the Native Americans were, in turn, finally defeated at the Battle of Wounded Knee.

You tell the story

Artists can create adventures in dreamed or imagined worlds, which would be difficult to express through words. Their poetic images invite us to invent stories of our own.

Rousseau was a self-taught French painter. He showed his work at the annual Paris show of artists that accepted pictures by painters like him. He was mocked for his simple vision, but believed himself to be a great artist. Rousseau drew from nature, in Paris, the botanic gardens, or the zoo. He combined the reality of what he saw with the equally vivid world of his imagination. This gives a dream-like feeling to his paintings.

A mysterious vision

This painting captures the innocence and strangeness of Rousseau's vision. The gypsy, the lion, the jug and the mandolin are all objects of the real world. Set together in this timeless, other-worldly landscape, they become mysterious. What can they be doing here? The gypsy's body, and the waving stripes on her rainbow-coloured robe, follow the contours of the desert sand. The lion stands out against the night sky like a statue. There is an atmosphere of eerie stillness.

❏ Henri Rousseau, **The Sleeping Gypsy (detail)**

Dream world

Rousseau uses smooth, careful brushwork and gives great attention to details such as the lion's mane and the gypsy's delicately painted feet – which shows his close observation of **reality**. But in some ways the scene is very unreal. Look at the odd way the gypsy and the mandolin are tilted towards the viewer, and the way the background is flattened, like a stage set.

❏ Henri Rousseau, **The Sleeping Gypsy (detail)**

- Do you think the lion is real or part of the gypsy's dream?
- Does the lion look fierce or friendly?
- Is the light harsh or soft? Where does it come from?
- What details catch the light?
- Imagine the gypsy's story. What do you think will happen next?

About the artists

The symbols below show the size and shape of the works shown in this book, compared with an average-sized adult.

Artemisia GENTILESCHI (page 15)

(1593-1652/3) Italian (Rome)
Judith and Maidservant with the Head of Holofernes, about 1625
Oil on canvas, 184.1 x 141.6 cm
© Detroit Institute of Arts, USA

Other works
❑ *Judith Beheading Holofernes*, 1618,
   Uffizi Gallery, Florence, Italy
❑ *Esther and Ahasuerus*, 1628-35
   Metropolitan Museum of Art, New York, USA
❑ *Self-portrait as the Allegory of Painting*, 1630s,
   Kensington Palace, London, UK

Luca GIORDANO (page 14)

(1634-1705) Italian (Naples)
Perseus Turning Phineas and His Followers to Stone, about 1680
Oil on canvas, 275 x 366 cm
National Gallery, London, UK

Other works
❑ *The Allegory of the Golden Fleece*, 1697
   Prado, Madrid, Spain
❑ *The Fall of the Rebel Angels*, 1666,
   Kunsthistorisches Musem, Vienna, Austria
❑ *Diana and Endymion*, 1675/80,
   National Gallery of Art, Washington DC, USA

Benozzo di Lese di Sandro GOZZOLI (pages 4-5)

(about 1420-97) Italian (Florence)
Dance of Salome, 1461/62
Tempera on panel, 23.8 x 34.5 cm
National Gallery of Art, Washington DC, USA

Other works
❑ *The Procession of the Three Kings*, 1459,
   Medici Chapel, Palazzo Riccardi, Florence, Italy
❑ *St Peter and Simon the Magus*,
   Metropolitan Museum of Art, New York, USA
❑ *The City of Babylon 1468-84*, Camposanto, Pisa, Italy

'Hergé' (Georges REMI) (page 9)

(1907-83) Belgian (Brussels)
The Calculus Affair, detail, page 25
Artwork © 1956, 1984 Casterman, text © 1960
Methuen Children's Books 1973 (English version)

Other works
❑ *The Black Island*, 1938, English version 1966
❑ *Tintin in America*, 1932, English version 1978
❑ *The Castafiore Emerald*, 1963, English version 1963

KESU SALAN and DHARMADAS (pages 12-13)

(Second half 16th century) Indian. Painters of the Court of Emperor Akbar
The Birth of Prince Salim, about 1590
Watercolour on paper, 32 x 18.9 cm
Victoria and Albert Museum, London, UK

Dorothea LANGE (pages 22-23)

(1895-1965) American (New Jersey)
Migrant Mother, Nipomo, California, 1936
(Full title: Destitute pea-pickers in California;
a 32 year old mother of seven children. February 1936)
Photograph (gelatin silver print), 34 x 27 cm (approx)
Oakland Museum, California, USA

Other works
❏ *Jobless on edge of pea field,* 1937,
  J.Paul Getty Museum, Los Angeles, USA
❏ *White Angel bread line,* 1933,
  George Eastman House, Rochester, USA
❏ *Cotton picker, Eloy,* 1940,
  Metropolitan Museum of Art, New York, USA

Robert Braithwaite MARTINEAU
(pages 16-17)

(1826-1869) English (London)
The Last Day in the Old Home, 1862
Oil on canvas, 107.3 x 144.8 cm
Tate Gallery, London, UK

Other works
❏ *Kit's First Writing Lesson,* 1852,
  Tate Gallery, London, UK
❏ *The Last Chapter,* 1863,
  Birmingham City Art Gallery and Museum, UK
❏ *Katherine and Petruchio,* 1855,
  Ashmolean Museum, Oxford, UK

Henri ROUSSEAU (pages 26-27)

(1844-1910) French (Lavel)
The Sleeping Gypsy, 1897
Oil on canvas, 129.5 x 200.7 cm
Museum of Modern Art, New York, USA

Other works
❏ *War,* 1894,
  Musée du Louvre, Paris, France
❏ *Tropical Forest with Monkeys,* 1910,
  National Gallery of Art, Washington DC, USA
❏ *Yadwiga's Dream,* 1910,
  Museum of Modern Art, New York, USA

Ousmane SOW (pages 24-25)

(1935-) Senegalese (Dakar)
The Battle of Little
*Big Horn,*1998
Mixed media,
group of 24 figures
and 11 horses, slightly larger than life-size
Collection of the artist

Other works
❏ *The Runner on the Starting Line,* 2001,
  Headquarters of Olympic Games Committee,
  Lausanne, Switzerland
❏ *Reclining Nouba* 1984,
  Museum of Troyes, France
❏ *The Wrestlers* 1984,
  Les Abattoirs Modern Art Museum, Toulouse, France

Grant WOOD (pages 20-21)

(1891-1942) American (Iowa)
Parson Weems' Fable, 1939
Oil on canvas, 97.5 x 127.3 cm
Amon Carter Museum, Fort Worth, Texas, USA (1970.43)

Other works

❏ *American Gothic*, 1930,
   Art Institute of Chicago, USA
❏ *Midnight Ride of Paul Revere*, 1931,
   Metropolitan Museum of Art, New York, USA
❏ *Death on the Ridge Road*, 1935,
   Williams College Museum of Art, Mass, USA

Joseph WRIGHT of Derby
(pages 18-19)

(1734-97) English (Derby)
An Experiment on a Bird in the Air Pump, 1768
Oil on canvas, 183 x 244 cm
National Gallery, London, UK

Other works

❏ *A Philosopher Lecturing with a Mechanical Planetary*, 1766,
   Derby Museum and Art Gallery, Derby, UK
❏ *The Blacksmith's Shop*, 1771,
   Yale Center for British Art, New Haven, CT, USA
❏ *An Eruption of Vesuvius*, 1774-76,
   The Huntington, San Marino, California USA

Unknown artists (pages 6-7)

Trajan's Column, Finished ad113
Marble, height 29.77 m (38 m with pedestal),
diameter 3.7 m.
Trajan's Forum, Rome, Italy

Unknown artists (page 8)

The Bayeux Tapestry (detail),
end 11th Century
Linen embroidered in wool,
50 cm x 70 m
William the Conquerer Centre, Bayeux, France

Unknown artist (pages 10-11)

The Life and Death of Sir Henry Unton,
about 1596
Oil on panel,
74 x 163.2 cm
National Portrait Gallery, London, UK

Glossary

Alcove A small space set back in a wall.

Ambassador A person who represents his country, or ruler, in another country.

Angle A position from which something is viewed.

Captions Titles or brief explanations added to pictures or cartoons.

Climax The most intense, exciting or important point of something.

Coat of arms A shield with symbols or pictures on it that is special to a person, family or country.

Composition The organization of the parts of a picture.

Court The people who live with and/or work for a ruler such as a king or queen.

Depression A slump or downturn in the economy of a country, when many people cannot find work. The Great Depression of the 1930s affected many countries around the world.

Diagonal Having a slanted direction.

Embroidered Sewn with thread or wool to make patterns or pictures.

Episodes A group of events that form part of a sequence.

Fable A story not founded on fact, often with a moral message.

Focal point The centre of interest or activity.

Fortifications Buildings or walls that are built to prevent an attack.

Forum A square or marketplace in an ancient Roman city, used for meetings and business.

Frame A single complete picture in a series of pictures.

Frieze A broad band of sculpture or painting.

Legend A story which comes from history, but which may not be true.

Miniature A small-scale, minutely finished painting, often in a book.

Native Americans A native person from America. Also sometimes called an American Indian.

Perspective A method of painting or drawing landscapes, figures and objects to make them appear three-dimensional.

Quiff A tuft of hair that points upwards.

Reality What really exists, rather than what is imagined.

Sequence A particular order in which pictures or events follow each other.

Sombre Dark or gloomy.

Still A photograph or a single shot from a film.

Tapestry Fabric with a design woven into it or stitched on to it.

War of Independence A war fought by the American colonies to win their independence from Great Britain (1775-83).

Widowed Become a widow (woman) or widower (man) because a husband or wife died.

Index

Numbers in **bold** show page numbers of illustrations